D1277937

OFFICIALLY WITHDRAWN
NEW HAVEN FREE PUBLIC LIBRARY

Color

The Scribbles Institute™ *Young Artist Basics*

Published by The Child's World®
PO Box 326
Chanhassen, MN 55317-0326
800-599-READ
www.childsworld.com

Printed in the United States of America

Design and Production: The Creative Spark, San Juan Capistrano, CA
Series Editor: Elizabeth Sirimarco Budd

Photos:
© Bob Krist/CORBIS: 19
© Corel Corporation: cover, 24, 25, 26, 27
© 2002 Artists Rights Society (ARS), New York/ADAGP, Paris/© Réunion des Musées Nationaux/Art Resource, NY: 12
© Fine Art Photographic Library, London/Art Resource, NY: 15
© Werner Forman/Art Resource, NY: 11
© Giraudon/Art Resource, NY: 30
© Erich Lessing/Art Resource, NY: 8, 21, 28, 29
© 2002 Estate of Pablo Picasso/Artists Rights Society (ARS), New York/© Réunion des Musées Nationaux/Art Resource, NY: 22
© 1998 Kate Rothko Prizel & Christopher Rothko/Artists Rights Society (ARS), New York/© Tate Gallery, London/Art Resource, NY: 16

Library of Congress Cataloging-in-Publication Data

Court, Rob, 1956–
Color / by Rob Court.
p. cm. — (Young artists basics series)
Includes index.
Summary: Simple text and "Loopi the Fantastic Line" describe the concept of color in art and architecture.
ISBN 1-56766-069-X (alk. paper)
1. Color in art—Juvenile literature. [1. Color. 2. Color in art.] I.Title. II. Series.
N7432.7 .C684 2002
701'.85—dc21

2002008013

Color

Rob Court

Loopi is a line,
a fantastic line.

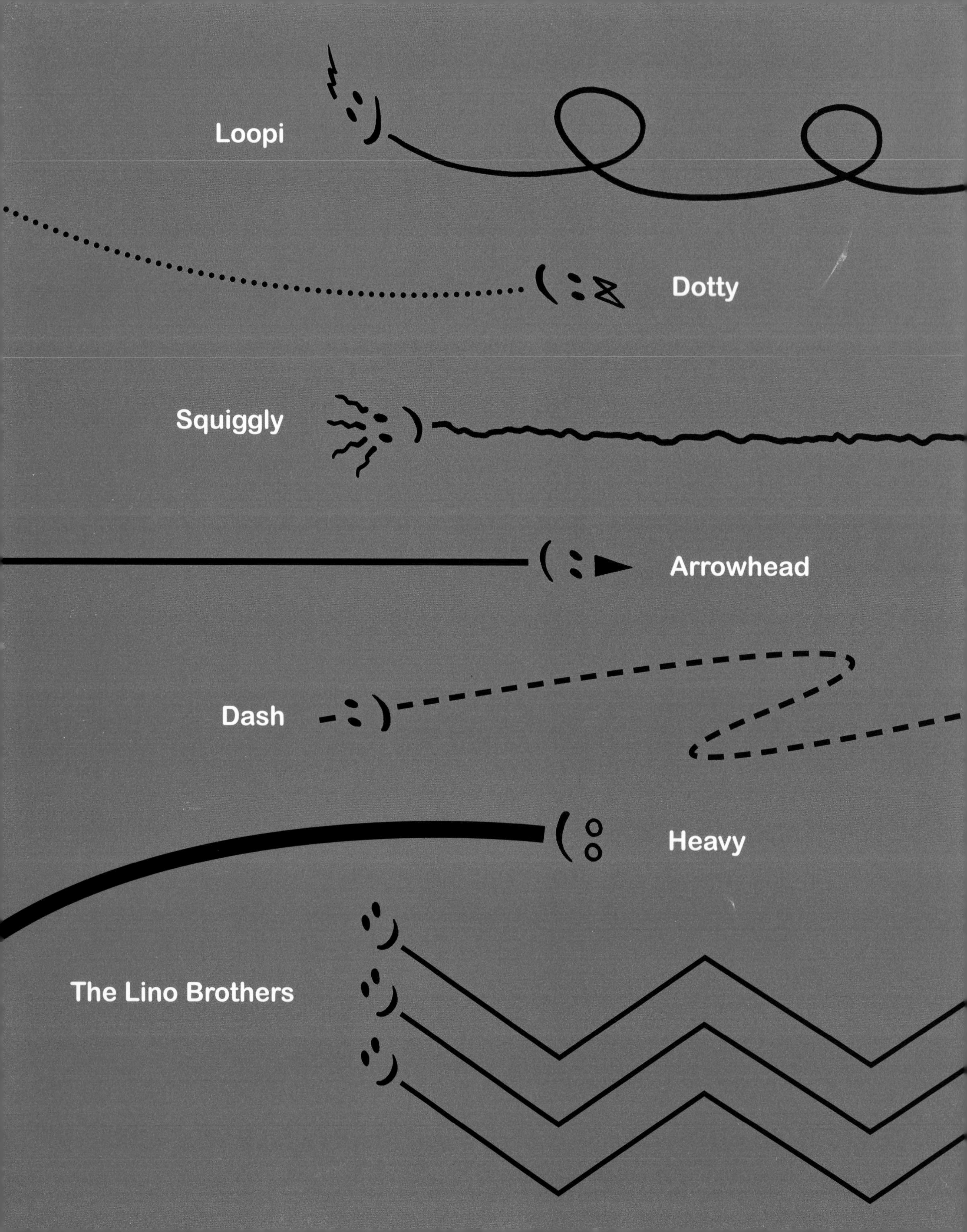
Loopi
Dotty
Squiggly
Arrowhead
Dash
Heavy
The Lino Brothers

There are many kinds of lines.

Some are dotted lines.

Some are squiggly lines.

Some lines point in a direction.

Some lines are drawn with dashes.

Other lines are very, very thick.

Sometimes lines work together
to help you understand color.

People have used color in artwork for thousands of years. Ancient Egyptians used color in pictures to tell stories.

When shapes and colors are repeated, they can make **patterns.** At left is a picture of a wall painting made in Egypt. It is 4,000 years old! Loopi shows you colorful patterns on the women's clothes. Can you find other patterns in the picture? What stories could the picture tell us?

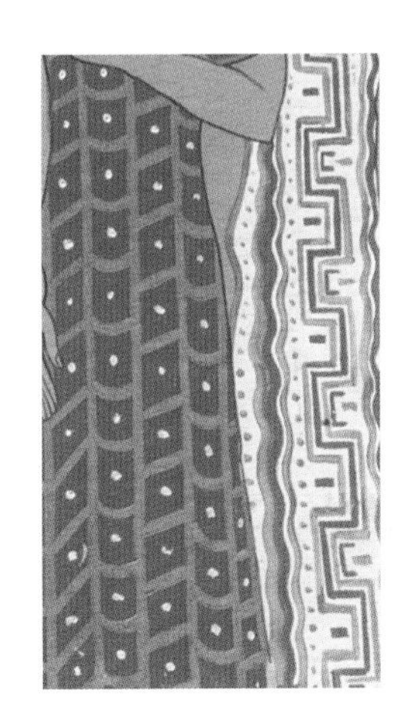

There are colors and patterns on this fabric from Peru. It is a blanket worn by an Inca long ago. The Inca were people who lived in South America hundreds of years ago. The blanket is more than 500 years old.

Below, Heavy shows you a rectangle. Rectangles have two long sides and two short sides. Look at the picture of the blanket. Can you find patterns made with rectangles and color? Can you name the colors in the picture?

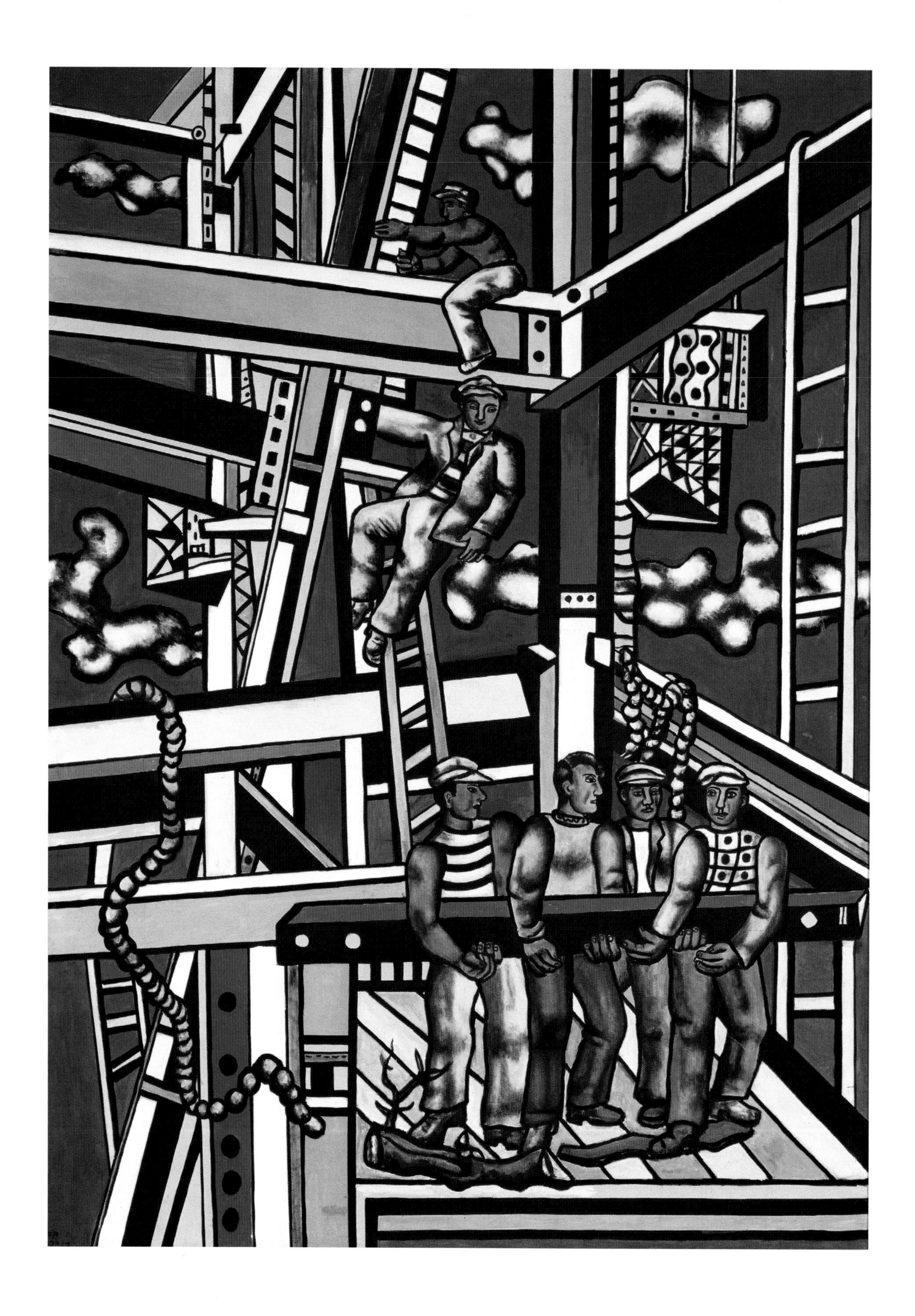

Artists can use red, yellow, and blue to create paintings. These three colors are the **primary colors.** Fernand Leger used primary colors in this painting of workers. He used black to paint **outlines.**

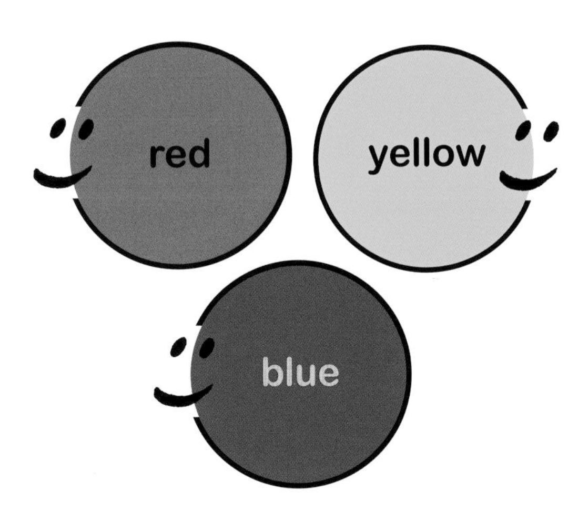

The Lino Brothers show you the primary colors. Can you find each color in Leger's painting? Do you see all three of the primary colors on the Inca blanket on page 11?

Left: Fernand Leger, *The Construction Workers*, 1950. Oil on canvas.

Light from the sun can help artists see different colors. They can paint colors that look like the real world.

This is a painting by James Tissot. Look closely. Can you find things that are red? Can you find Dotty? She points out shadows on the umbrella. They are dark red. Can you find other shadows in the picture? How did Tissot use color to create shadows?

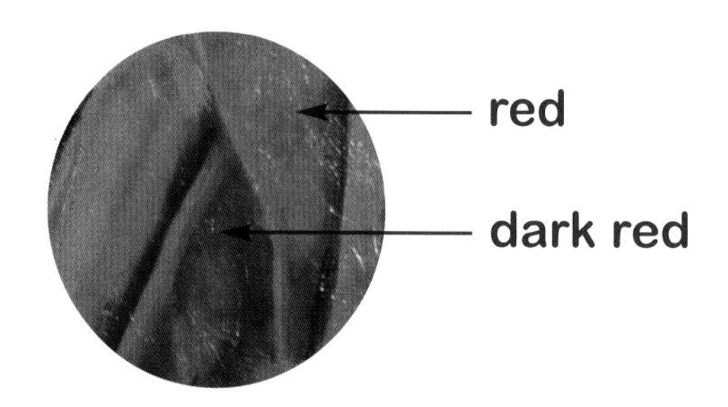

Right: James Tissot, *A Special Outing*, c. 1860. Oil on canvas.

Nicolas de Stael, *Sicily,* date unknown. Oil on canvas.

Art that does not look like the real world is called **abstract art.** At left is an abstract painting by Nicolas de Stael. He mixed red with white to make light red.

Look at de Stael's painting. Dash shows you an area where red paint is mixed with white. Can you find other areas of this painting where red is mixed with white?

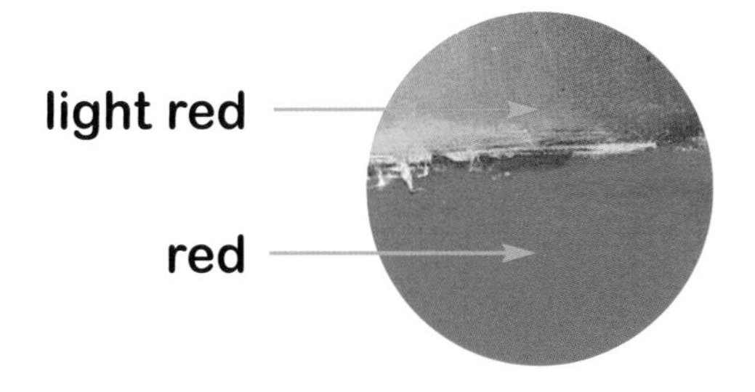

This big yellow fish is a **sculpture** in the country of Thailand. Some areas of yellow look darker where light does not shine.

Can you find Dotty in the picture? She helps you see light and dark yellow on the sculpture. Is there a pattern on the fish's body? Are there other primary colors in the picture?

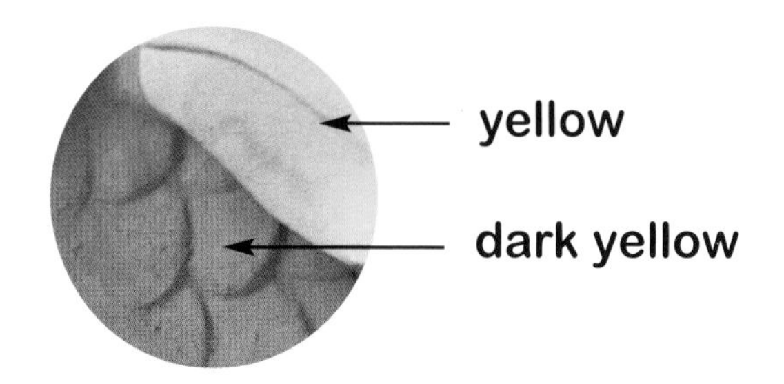

日月光華
普救眾生
壽康
富貴
大吉

Artists can choose colors that express their feelings.

Vincent van Gogh painted this **self-portrait.** He used the color blue to express his feelings. In this picture, do you think he feels happy or sad?

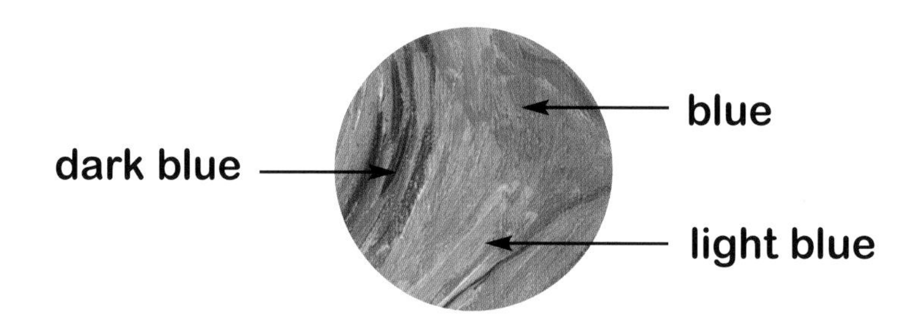

Study van Gogh's self-portrait. Can you see areas where he mixed white with blue? What other colors do you see?

Right: Vincent van Gogh, *Self-portrait*, 1889. Oil on canvas.

Artists can mix colors when they paint. Two primary colors mixed together make a **secondary color.**

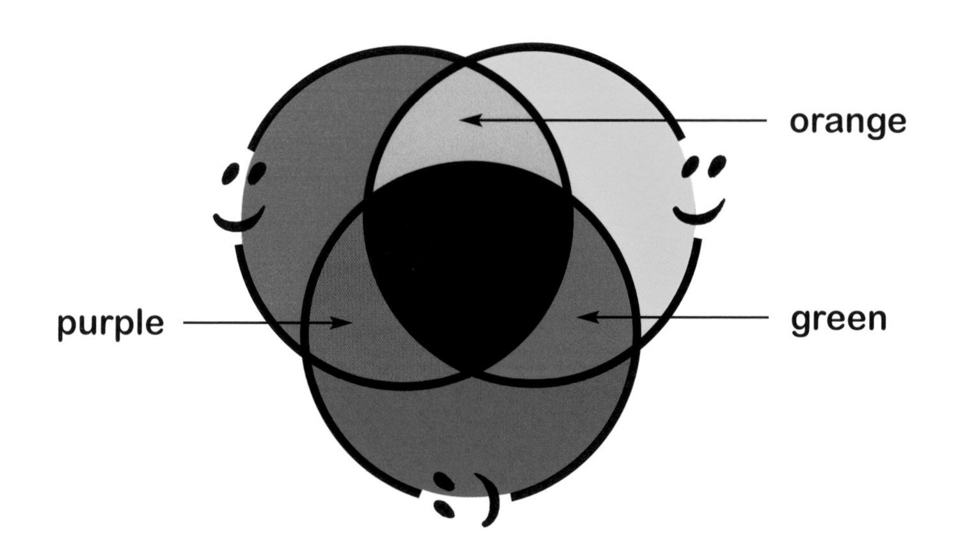

The Lino Brothers show you secondary colors. They are orange, green, and purple. Pablo Picasso created the painting at left. It is a **portrait** of a woman. Can you find secondary colors in the portrait?

Left: Pablo Picasso, *Portrait of Dora Maar*, 1937. Oil on canvas.

You can see color in nature. Animals have natural colors that can blend into the colors around them.

Below is a picture of a bird with her babies. The colors of her feathers blend in with the colors around her. Why is it important for a bird's colors to look like other colors around it? Do you see green in the picture? Do you see a primary color?

The bright colors of flowers create wonderful patterns. When colors look pretty together, we say they are in harmony with each other.

Loopi shows you the colors of a flower. Can you see primary colors in the picture? Are there patterns in the picture?

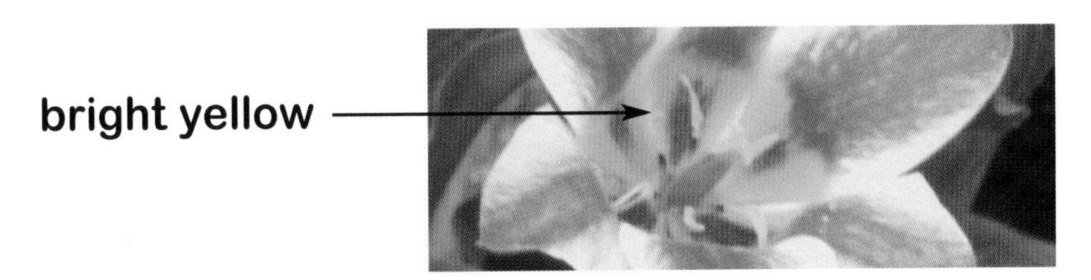

Some colors look warm. They are called warm colors.

Dash shows you the warm colors of a canyon. Can you see red and yellow in the picture? Can you find warm colors in the painting by van Gogh on page 21?

Some colors look cool. They are called cool colors.

Dash shows you the cool colors of a wintery day. Can you see blue and white? If you could touch the snow, how would it feel? Can you find cool colors in van Gogh's painting?

This **landscape** was painted by Claude Monet. Natural color and light are important in Monet's artwork.

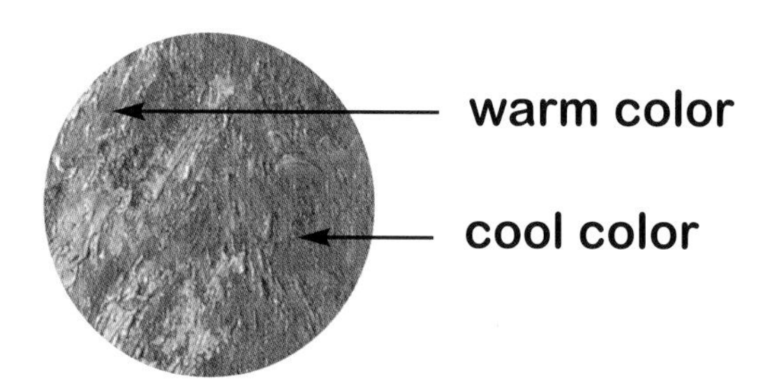

He mixed warm and cool colors to create shadows and **texture** on stacks of hay.

Claude Monet, *The Haystacks, End of Summer*, 1891. Oil on canvas.

Monet painted these colors as he saw them in real life. Dotty shows you where he mixed warm and cool colors to make shadows. Can you find other shadows and colors in the picture?

Paul Gauguin, *Ta Matete,* 1892. Gouache on canvas.

This painting was created by Paul Gauguin. It is a colorful picture of people on the island of Tahiti. He used brown for the color of their skin. You can create brown by mixing all three primary colors together.

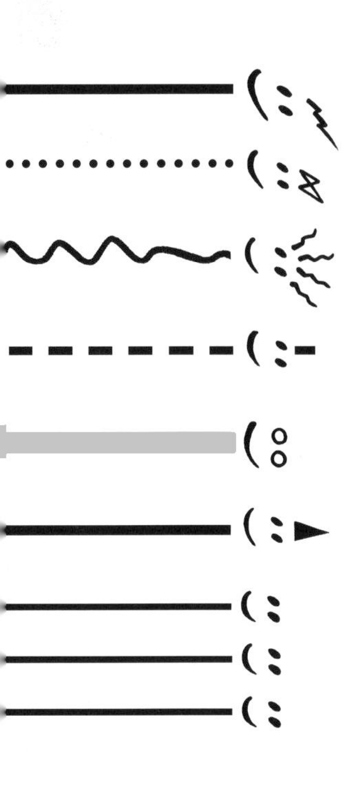

Put It All Together

Take a minute to study the painting by Gauguin. The women are wearing bright clothing. Can you see primary colors on their dresses? Can you see secondary colors? Which colors did Gauguin choose to paint trees in the background? You can create a picture of your family or friends. Choose from primary or secondary colors for their clothes.

Create a Colorful Portrait

Try making a portrait of someone special. Remember, the portrait can be of yourself! Do you remember van Gogh's self-portrait on page 21? Do you remember Picasso's portrait of a woman on page 22? These paintings can give you many ideas for creating a portrait. You can express how you feel! Choose from all of the colors you've learned about here.

Students, Teachers, and Parents

LOOPI the Fantastic Line™ is always waiting to help you learn more about drawing with color—at **www.scribblesinstitute.com**. You can get helpful ideas for your drawings at the Scribbles Institute™. It's a great place for students, teachers, and parents to find books, information, and tips about drawing. You can even get advice from a drawing coach!

Glossary

abstract art (AB-strakt ART)
Abstract art uses color, shape, and movement to express ideas and feelings. It does not have to represent objects or people exactly as they look in the real world.

landscape (LAND-skayp)
A landscape is a picture showing a view of scenery or the land.

outlines (OWT-lynz)
Outlines are lines that show the shape of an object. A drawing done in outlines shows only an object's outer lines.

patterns (PAT-ternz)
Patterns are designs made with repeated shapes and colors. You can find patterns on fabric, wrapping paper, or wallpaper, for example.

portrait (POR-trit)
A portrait is a work of art that represents a real person.

primary colors (PRY-mayr-ee KULL-erz)
Primary colors are the colors that, when mixed together, can produce all other colors. Red, yellow, and blue are the primary colors.

sculpture (SKULP-cher)
A sculpture is a work of art formed into a shape to represent something. Sculptures can be carved from stone or made from metal.

secondary color (SEK-un-dayr-ee KULL-er)
A secondary color is created by mixing primary colors together. For example, mixing blue and yellow creates green.

self-portrait (SELF POR-trit)
A self-portrait is a work of art created by an artist that shows himself or herself.

texture (TEKS-cher)
How a surface feels when you touch it is called texture. The texture of an apple is smooth, for example.

Index

About the Author
Rob Court is a designer and illustrator. He has a studio in San Juan Capistrano, California. He started the Scribbles Institute™ to help people learn about the importance of drawing and creativity.

This book is dedicated to Jesse and Jasmine.